for Mike and Sam

Copyright © 1996 by Steve Lavis

First published in the United States in 1997
by Lodestar Books, an affiliate of Dutton Children's Books,
a division of Penguin Books USA Inc.
Originally published in Great Britain in 1996
by Ragged Bears Limited, Hampshire, England.

Printed in Singapore   ISBN 0-525-67542-6
First American Edition   10 9 8 7 6 5 4 3 2 1

Cock-a-doodle-doo

A Farmyard Counting Book
by Steve Lavis

Lodestar Books

Dutton   New York

COCK

1 One noisy rooster

a-doodle-doo

waking up the farm

Neigh

2 Two hungry horses

Neigh

waiting to be fed

Moo

3 Three sleepy cows

MOO

going to be milked

Woof Woof

4 Four frisky dogs

Woof

looking for some fun

Oink Oink

5 Five pink pigs

Oink

playing in the mud

Quack

6 Six waddling ducks

Quack

Quack

off for a swim

Baa

7 Seven woolly sheep

Baa

wandering to and fro

8 Eight playful cats

meow

chasing a mouse

squeak

9 Nine nimble mice

Squeak Squeak

Squeak Squeak

stealing a snack

Cluck Cluck

10 Ten clucking chickens

Cluck Cluck

roosting in the barn

And they all live...

together

Quack Woof

Woof Cock-a-doodle

Meow

Cock-a-doodle Baa Neigh

on one very...

doo Cluck Oink

Meow Baa

squeak Moo

Cluck Quack

NOISY farm.